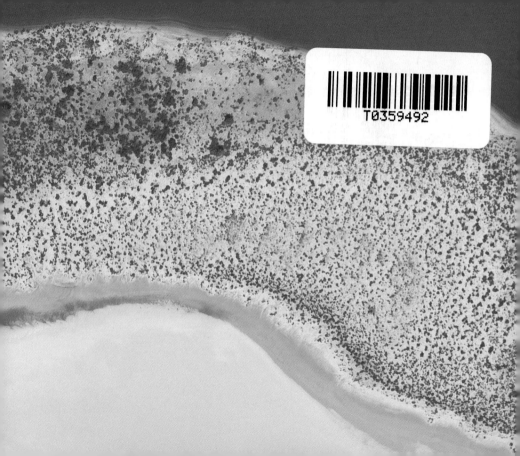

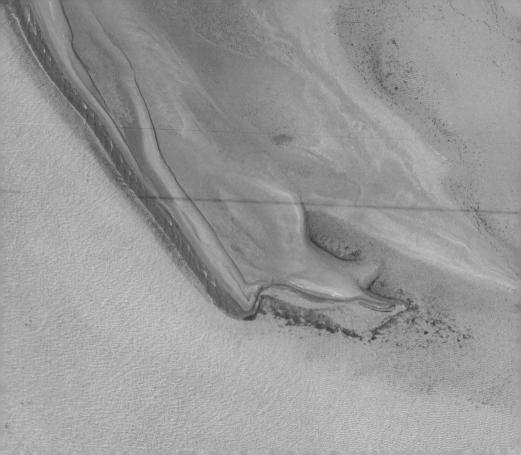

THE AUSTRALIAN OUTBACK

THE AUSTRALIAN

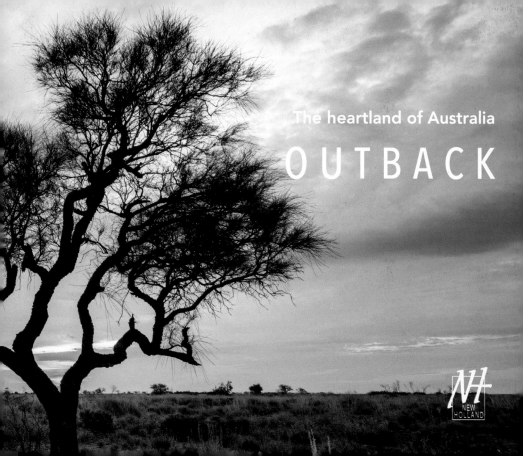

The heartland of Australia

OUTBACK

NEW HOLLAND

THE AUSTRALIAN OUTBACK

The Australian Outback comprises vast remoteness and sparsely populated regions outside of the major cities and towns around Australia, and is often a remote and isolated place to live or visit.

It is rich in cultural roots with significant Aboriginal sites, the traditional owners of the land, whose culture and traditions are active across Australia with over 60,000 years of Australian history.

There are many natural wonders in the outback including stargazing and incredible sunsets, with waterholes, secret caves, native wildlife, and the most breathtaking views across landscapes as far as the eye can see.

People living in remote towns and communities are involved in tourism, farming and agriculture, as well as cattle and sheep stations or work in the mines, and may often have to travel hundreds, sometimes thousands, of kilometres to buy their groceries see a doctor or hospital.

The weather is generally hot and dry with no underground water or rivers, and can be a difficult place to adapt to, living in this rugged environment with either floods or drought. Most people living in the outback were either born there or move to outback regions due to work. Around 5% of the Australian population live in the outback.

THE BEAUTY OF
THE OUTBACK

THE BEAUTY OF THE OUTBACK

The Australian outback features rugged wilderness, natural landscapes, historical and cultural richness, vast red earth, unique flora and fauna, starry night skies, and breathtaking sunrises and sunsets.

The endless horizons of nature and its true beauty make the land truly unique with much to offer from dawn to dusk.

The beauty of the Australian outback is the vastness of space where you can just

be with nature watching sunsets over mountain ranges or seeing unique wildlife from birds around waterholes or kangaroos in their natural environment along with camels, goats, horses, reptiles and lots of wildlife some only found in the outback. With breath taking night skies that show the vast landscape at sunset and the evening night sky that is sheer beauty which can only be found in the remote outback.

While it can be the most remote and extreme places on planet earth it is some of the most beautiful and peaceful places that one can ever find themselves in with so much beauty surrounding you that the Australian outback is like no other place.

Alice Springs, Northern Territory.

Kata Tjuta / Mount Olga, Northern Territory.

Road in the Outback.

Sturt Stony Desert, South Australia.

A red dirt-roads in the Karijini National Park in Western Australia.

Karlu Karlu / Devils Marbles, Warumungu, Northern Territory.

Bald Rock National Park, northern New South Wales.

Girraween National Park, Darling Downs, Queensland.

Kata Tjuta / Mount Olga, Northern Territory.

Mount Kaputar National Park, New South Wales.

The Pinnacles, Nambung National Park, Western Australia.

Ghost gum eucalyptus.

Kata Tjuta / The Olgas. Northern Territory, central Australia.

Outback Wave Rock in Hyden, Western Australia. This rock formation looks like a tall breaking ocean wave.

Red dirt road in the Outback.

Flinders Ranges, South Australia.

Coober Pedy, South Australia.

Sheep farm in outback Victoria.

Outback wilderness and remoteness.

Kati Thanda / Lake Eyre in South Australia.

Railway track near Broken Hill, New South Wales.

Flinders Ranges National Park, South Australia.

Outback thunder storm.

Glen Helen Gorge water hole, Finke River, Northern Territory.

Lake Argyle, near the Kimberley region, Western Australia.

Open road.

Kangaroo warning sign.

Kimberley, Western Australia.

Nitmiluk / Katherine Gorge, Northern Territory.

Leliyn / Edith Falls, Katherine, Northern Territory.

Knox Lookout, Karijini National Park, Western Australia.

Lake Argygle at Kimberley, Western Australia.

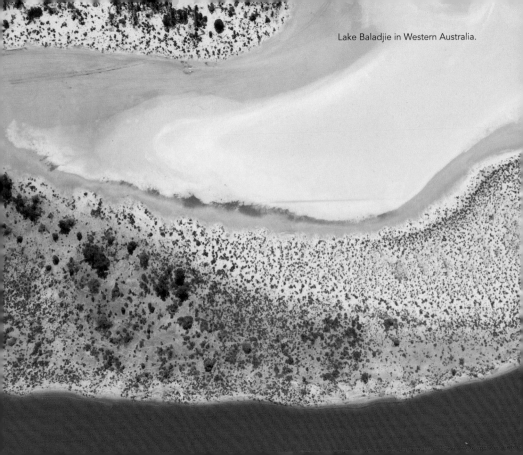

Lake Baladjie in Western Australia.

Outback roads.

The Milky Way found in Australia's outback.

Natures Window in Kalbarri National Park, Western Australia.

Niagara Dam Nature Reserve in Kookynie, Western Australia.

Tjoritja / West MacDonnell National Park, Northern Territory.

Tjoritja / West MacDonnell National Park, Northern Territory.

Outback sunset.

Lake Ballard salt lake, Western Australia.

Limestone formations within Nambung National Park, Western Australia.

Ellery Creek Big Hole waterhole in West MacDonnell Ranges.

Sunset at the Big Red Sand Dune /
Nappanerica, Simpson Desert, Queensland.

Purnululu National Park, Western Australia.

Simpsons Gap, West MacDonnell Ranges, Northern Territory.

Rainbow in the outback desert

Rainbow Valley, Northern Territory.

Sunset in the Outback.

Sunrise in the Outback.

Rugged peaks of Flinders Ranges mountains in South Australia.

Fence in Queensland.

Rest stop.

Sunrise in the Outback.

Uluru-Kata Tjura National Park, Northern Territory.

Camel crossing sign warning drive in Northern Territory.

Karlu Karlu / Devils Marbles Conservation Reserve.

Waterhole in the Northern Territory.

Uluru.

Uluru.

Railway Crossing in the Outback.

Rainbow Valley, Northern Territory.

Simpsons Gap, MacDonnell Ranges.

Outback waterhole.

Big Red Sand Dune / Nappanerica, Simpson Desert, Queensland.

The red earth of the Kalgoorlie landscape, Western Australia.

Gammon Ranges, South Australia.

People swimming at Mataranka hot pools in the Northern Territory.

Starry night sky over outback landscape.

Sunset reflections on Lake Menindee, Darling River, New South Wales.

Sunset on the open road.

Sunrise in Karijini National Park in Western Australia.

Outback Highway.

The Outback Highway passing through Flinders Ranges at dusk.

Ormiston Gorge Alice Springs, Northern Territory.

Milky Way arching over El Questro National Park in Western Australia.

Desert sunsets.

Flinders Ranges at sunset.

Track across outback.

Mungo National Park, NSW.

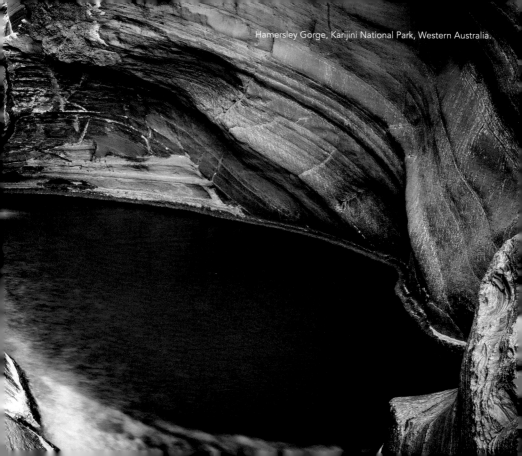

Hamersley Gorge, Karijini National Park, Western Australia.

The Breakaways, Coober Pedy, South Australia.

Dirt road across the Pilbara, Western Australian

AUSTRALIAN WILDLIFE

AUSTRALIAN WILDLIFE

The Australian outback is home to a wide variety of fascinating animals, from the most iconic kangaroo to wallabies and koalas.

There is also a rich breed of parrots and bird life in the outback as well as deadly snakes, reptiles and lizards, and even some frogs that are only found in the outback.

Also in the Australian deserts, you will find many other animals like dingos, goats, camels, bats, crocodiles, snakes, and spiders with over 500 different species of wildlife found in the Australian outback.

Not to be forgotten is the spiny echidna, a curious egg-laying mammal that scuttles about in search of ants and termites. Each of these animals plays a vital role in the delicate ecosystem of the Australian outback, creating a symphony of life amidst the rugged beauty of this ancient land.

Exploring the vast desert, hearing native birds at dawn, and seeing kangaroos hopping across the red desert, for nature and wildlife lovers, there is simply no place quite like the Australian outback to immerse yourself in the wonders of the natural world.

Thorny Devil (*Moloch horridus*).

Dingo, Australia's wild dog.

Red Kangaroo (*Macropus rufus*).

Brolgas (*Antigone rubicunda*).

Camel.

Echidna.

Camels amid termite mounds.

Galahs (*Eolophus roseicapilla*).

White cattle in the Northern Territory.

Saltwater Crocodile (*Crocodylus porosus*).

Emus (*Dromaius novaehollandiae*).

Bilby (*Macrotis lagotis*).

Laughing Kookaburra (*Dacelo novaeguineae*).

Koala *(Phascolarctos cinereus).*

Goanna (*Varanus caudolineatus*).

Frilled-neck Lizard (*Chlamydosaurus kingii*).

Thorny Devil (*Moloch horridus*).

Central Bearded Dragon (*Pogona vitticeps*).

Woma Python (*Aspidites ramsayi*).

Stimson's Python (*Antaresia stimsoni*).

A black and orange Australian Ringed Brown Snake on the red desert sand.

Australian Bearded Dragon.

Perentie (*Varanus giganteus*).

Shingleback Lizard (*Tiliqua rugosa*).

Eastern Rosella (*Platycercus eximius*).

Yellow-tailed Black Cockatoo (*Zanda funerea*).

Wedge-tailed Eagle (*Aquila audax*).

Galahs (*Eolophus roseicapilla*).

Major Mitchell's Cockatoo (Cacatua leadbeateri)

Spinifex Hopping Mouse (*Notomys alexis*)

Gray-headed Flying Fox (*Pteropus poliocephalus*).

Long-nosed Potoroo (*Potorous tridactylus*).

Fat-tailed Dunnart (*Sminthopsis crassicaudata*).

Blue-winged Kookaburra (*Dacelo leachii*).

Sturt's Desert Pea (*Swainsona formosa*).

Bull Banksia *(Banksia grandis)*.

Gum leaves (*Eucalyptus*).

Mulla Mulla (*Ptilotus exaltatus*) flowers.

Bush Tomato (*Solanum*).

Grevillea juncifolia in the Red Centre.

Sea Lavender (*Limonium sinuatum*).

Prickly Pears (*Opuntia* sp.) tree.

THE LIFESTYLE, HOMES, TOWNS AND THE UNIQUE

THE LIFESTYLE, HOMES, TOWNS AND THE UNIQUE

The lifestyle, homes, towns, and the unique landscapes of the Australian outback are truly one of a kind. In the vast expanse of the outback, you'll find a resilient community of people who have adapted to the harsh environment, creating a way of life that is both challenging and rewarding.

The homes in the outback range from traditional homesteads to modern eco-friendly designs that blend seamlessly with the surrounding nature. Each town you come across

tells a story of survival and perseverance, with locals who were either born there, there for work in the outback or want to live outside of the larger cities,

People feel a sense of freedom living in open spaces and a connection to the land with sunrises and sunsets that are breathtaking to live amongst. Where time moves more slowly allowing people to live with a more simplistic lifestyle and neighbours come together to support each other during tough times.

With its rich Aboriginal culture that has thrived in the region for thousands of years with ancient rock art, dreamtime stories and traditional practices of the Aboriginal people that provide a deep connection to the land and its spiritual significance.

Grindell's Hut in the Vulkathunha / Gammon Ranges National Park, South Australia.

Stockman.

Herd of cattle

Abandoned car alongside remains of ruined 19th century stone house.

Farmer on quad bike mustering cattle.

Abandoned railway carriage in the remote South Australian outback town of Cook.

Lightning Ridge, New South Wales.

Trucks in the outback.

Cottage in Kalgoorlie, Western Australia.

Coolamine Homestead, Kosciuszko
National Park New South Wales.

Cattle station in the outback.

Hillside entrance to a dug out, an underground house in the opal mining town of Coober Pedy, South Australia.

Tennant Creek Telegraph Station, Northern Territory.

Home in Western Australia.

Old rusty tin in Narloo, Western Australia.

Windmill.

Planting sorghum during sunset on a farm.

Relaxing in a hammock.

Railtrack in the Outback.

Railway track through the outback from Adelaide to Darwin.

Australian outback at night.

Cobar, central western New South Wales.

Tibooburra, north western New South Wales.

Darling River around remote Wilcannia, New South Wales.

Coober Pedy, an opal mining town in the red center desert where many houses are underground.

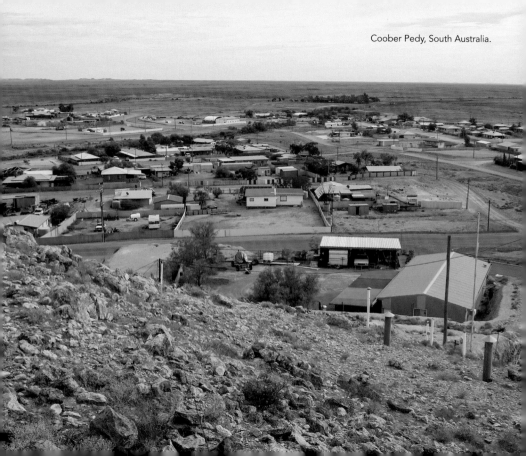
Coober Pedy, South Australia.

Coober Pedy.

Hillside entrance to a dug out, an underground house in Coober Pedy.

Coober Pedy.

Alice Springs.

Alice Springs.

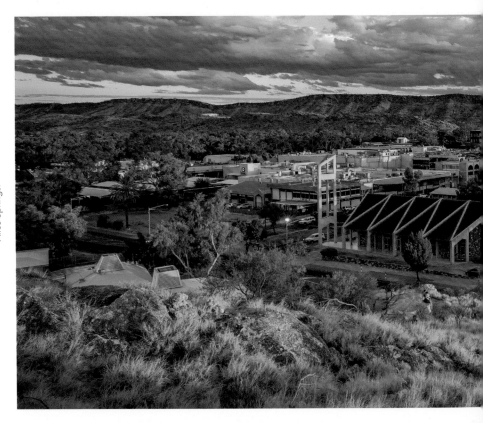

Alice Springs.

Road sign in Northern Territory.

Truck sign.

Battery Hill Mining in Tennant Creek, Northern Territory.

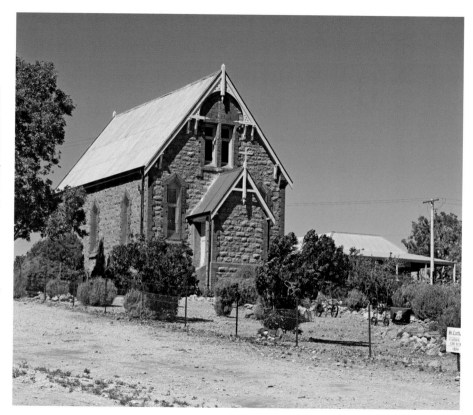

St Carthage's Catholic Church, Silverton, New South Wales.

Opal mining at Lightning Ridge, New South Wales.

Abandoned underground mine entrances at Lightning Ridge, New South Wales.

Church at Lightning Ridge, New South Wales.

Lightning Ridge sunset.

Beer can wall.

The ghost town of Silverton, New South Wales.

Silverton Hotel, New South Wales.

Mad Max 2 Museum,
Silverton.

Silverton Hotel.

Silverton, north-west of Broken Hill, New South Wales.

Silverton, New South Wales.

Skyline sunsets.

Old mine site, Broken Hill.

Broken Hill, New South Wales.

Metal ore on freight trains at Broken Hill train station.

Broken HIll Miners Memorial.

Outback sheep station near Broken Hill.

The Broken Hill Sculptures

The outback opal mining town of White Cliffs.

White Cliffs, New South Wales.

Hawker, near Flinders Ranges, South Australia.

The Marree Hotel, South Australia.

Long Reach Railway Station, Queensland.

Sunset along the Thomson River in Longreach.

Mildura, northwest Victoria.

South Australian outback.

Palae theatre in Kalgorlie, mining town in Western Australia.

Super Pit, Kalgoorlie, Western Australia.

Kalgoorlie–Boulder, Western Australia.

Replica of Paddy Hannan Statue outside the Town Hall, Kalgoorlie, Western Australia.

Historic buildings of the city of Kalgoorlie, Western Australia.

Main street at Kalgoorlie–Boulder, Western Australia.

Pink Roadhouse, Oodnadatta, South Australia.

The remote South Australian town of Innamincka.

Recycled pedestrian sign.

Newman, outback mining town in the Pilbara region of Western Australia.

Sunset in Glendambo, a rural desert village in central Australia.

Tennant Creek Telegraph Station Historical Reserve, Northern Territory.

Battery Hill Gold Mine Museum of Tennant Creek.

Birdsville Hotel, Queensland near South Australia.

The Carcory Ruins can be seen just outside the outback town of Birdsville.

Blinman,

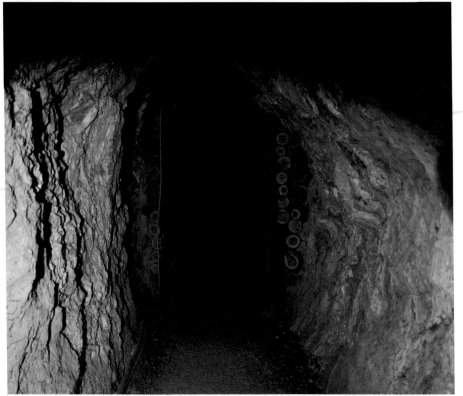

Old underground tunnel, Blinman, South Australia.

The town of Blinman in the Flinders Ranges of South Australia.

Winton in Central West Queensland.

Road passing through Carrieton, South Australia.

Camp oven cook fest, a banquet Charleville, south Western Queensland.

Kimba, South Australia.

The Katherine River and the town of Katherine, Northern Territory.

Wyandra, Queensland.

Outback toilets.

Vintage wooden wagon abandoned in the outback.

The outback town of Windorah, Queensland.

The far outback town of Cunnamulla, Queensland.

Mc Kinlay, Queensland.

Silverton Cemetery, New South Wales.

Barbecue and picnic area in Western Australia.

The outback town of Tambo, western Queensland.

The far western town of Eula, Queensland.

Newman Town.

Solar dishes outside town of Windorah, Queensland.

grain silo and sheds at Shepherds Geelong, Victoria.

Wilcannia, New South Wales.

Public toilet building also known as the Dunny.

Outback playground.

Wind wheel at Gnaraloo Station, Western Australia.

Letterboxes in the Outback.

An historic landmark in Alice Springs, Northern Territory.

Trucks in the Outback.

THE AUSTRALIAN STOCKMAN'S HALL OF FAME
AND OUTBACK HERITAGE CENTRE

Australian Stockman's Hall of Fame, Longreach, Queensland.

Trades Hall, Broken Hill, western New South Wales.

William Creek Hotel, Oodnadatta Track, William Creek, South Australia.

An outback road, Western Australia.

Solar panel field.

First published in 2024 by New Holland Publishers
Sydney

Level 1, 178 Fox Valley Road, Wahroonga, NSW 2076, Australia

newhollandpublishers.com

A record of this book is held at the National Library of Australia.

ISBN 9781760796785

Managing Director: Fiona Schultz
Designer: Andrew Davies
Production Director: Arlene Gippert
Printed in China

10 9 8 7 6 5 4 3 2 1

Keep up with New Holland Publishers:

◼ NewHollandPublishers

◯ @newhollandpublishers

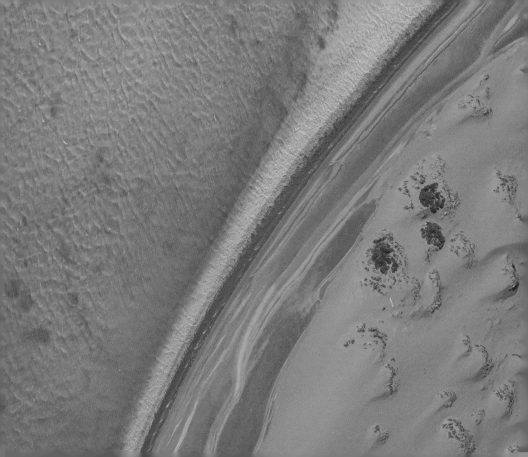

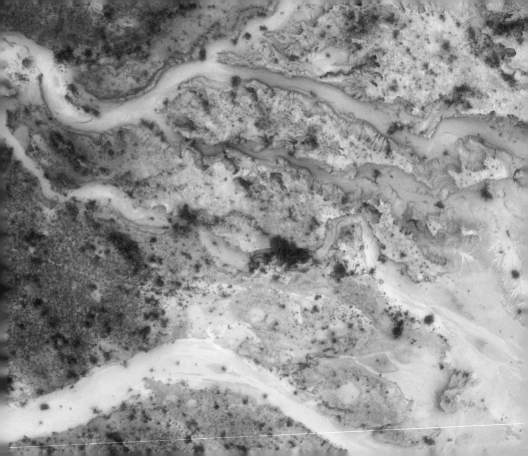